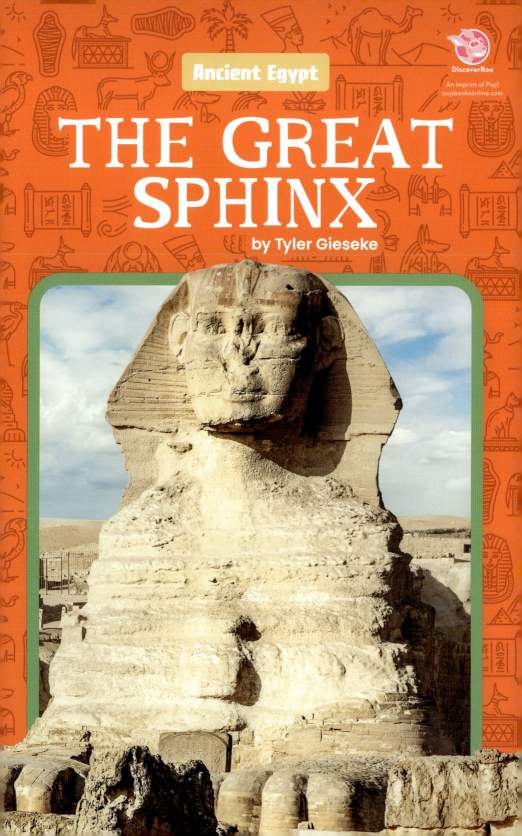

Ancient Egypt

THE GREAT SPHINX

by Tyler Gieseke

abdobooks.com

Published by Pop!, a division of ABDO, PO Box 398166, Minneapolis, Minnesota 55439. Copyright ©2022 by Abdo Consulting Group, Inc. International copyrights reserved in all countries. No part of this book may be reproduced in any form without written permission from the publisher. DiscoverRoo™ is a trademark and logo of Pop!.

Printed in the United States of America, North Mankato, Minnesota.

052021
092021

THIS BOOK CONTAINS RECYCLED MATERIALS

Cover Photos: Shutterstock Images
Interior Photos: Shutterstock Images, 1, 6–7, 11, 14–15, 19–20, 23, 26–29; iStockphoto, 5, 8, 24; Werner Forman Archive/Shutterstock, 12; Metropolitan Museum of Art, 17

Editor: Elizabeth Andrews
Series Designer: Laura Graphenteen

Library of Congress Control Number: 2020948925
Publisher's Cataloging-in-Publication Data

Names: Gieseke, Tyler, author.
Title: The great Sphinx / by Tyler Gieseke.
Description: Minneapolis, Minnesota : Pop!, 2022 | Series: Ancient Egypt | Includes online resources and index.
Identifiers: ISBN 9781532169908 (lib. bdg.) | ISBN 9781644945384 (pbk.) | ISBN 9781098240837 (ebook)
Subjects: LCSH: Great Sphinx (Egypt)--Juvenile literature. | Sphinxes (Mythology)--Juvenile literature. | Egypt--Antiquities--Juvenile literature. | Egypt--History--Juvenile literature.
Classification: DDC 932.01--dc23

Pop open this book and you'll find QR codes loaded with information, so you can learn even more!

Scan this code* and others like it while you read, or visit the website below to make this book pop!

popbooksonline.com/great-sphinx

*Scanning QR codes requires a web-enabled smart device with a QR code reader app and a camera.

TABLE OF CONTENTS

CHAPTER 1
The Great Sphinx 4

CHAPTER 2
A Lion of Limestone 10

CHAPTER 3
Sphinxes Rule .16

CHAPTER 4
A World Symbol 22

Making Connections. 30
Glossary 31
Index. 32
Online Resources 32

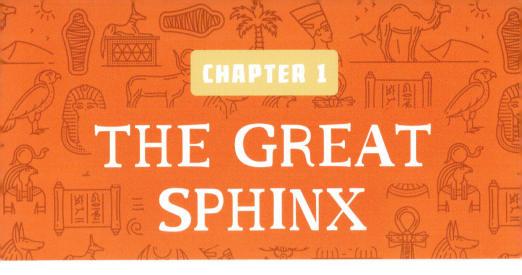

CHAPTER 1
THE GREAT SPHINX

A giant animal lies watchfully in front of a **pyramid** near Giza, Egypt. The animal has the body of a lion and the head of a man. It has sat there for more than 4,000 years.

WATCH A VIDEO HERE!

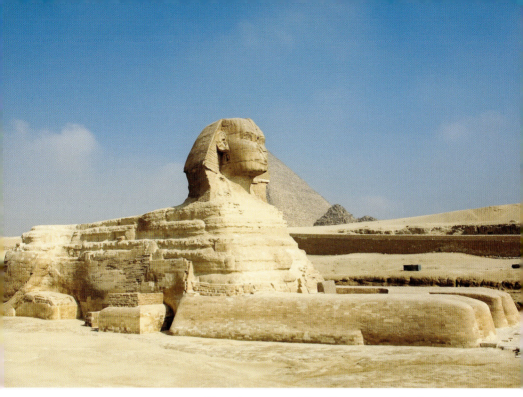

The Great Sphinx has a curled tail and four paws, all made of stone.

The animal is really a **statue**. But, it has sparked fear and respect in people who have seen it. The statue is known around the world. It is the Great Sphinx!

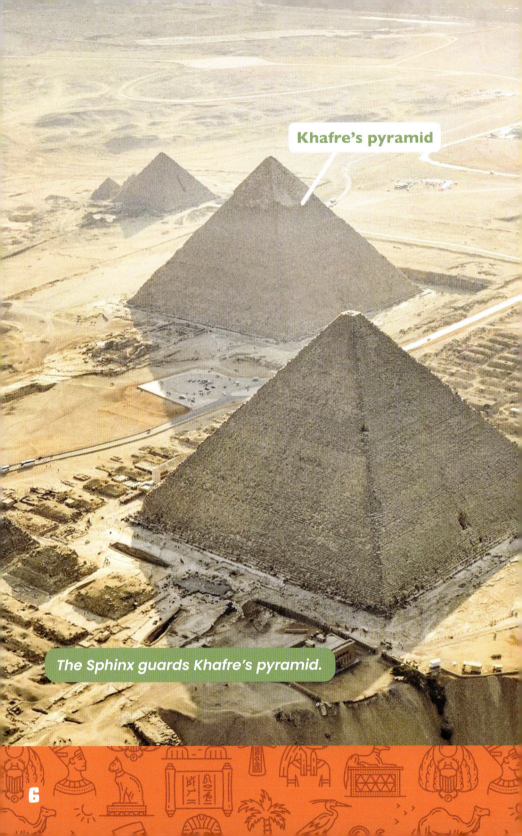

Ancient Egyptians created the Great Sphinx early in Egypt's history. They finished it while Khafre was **pharaoh**. Khafre ruled from 2520 to 2494 BCE. Many scientists believe the Sphinx's head is meant to look like Khafre's.

DID YOU KNOW?

Khafre ruled during the Old Kingdom. This was very early in Egyptian history.

The heads of these ancient Egyptian sphinx statues show the pharaoh Nekhtanebo.

The Great Sphinx sits near three famous pyramids. The biggest of these was a **tomb** for Khafre's father, Khufu. It is known as the Great Pyramid of Giza.

The second-biggest pyramid was Khafre's tomb. The Great Sphinx is in front of this pyramid. The smallest pyramid was a tomb for Khafre's son, Menkaure.

Sphinxes were common in ancient Egyptian art. They **symbolized** power. Societies in Greece and Asia built sphinx statues too. The Great Sphinx became a global symbol of wealth and command.

The Pyramids of Giza are one of the Seven Wonders of the Ancient World.

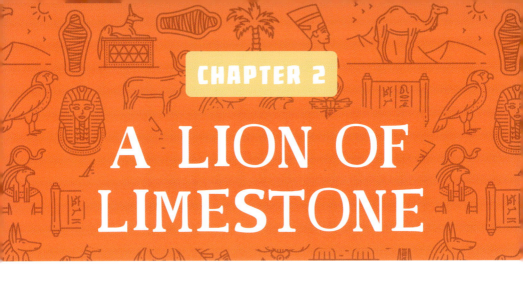

CHAPTER 2
A LION OF LIMESTONE

The Great Sphinx was originally made of a single piece of limestone. Limestone is a soft type of rock. It is easy to carve. Even though it is soft, limestone can last many years.

LEARN MORE HERE!

People have restored the Great Sphinx several times.

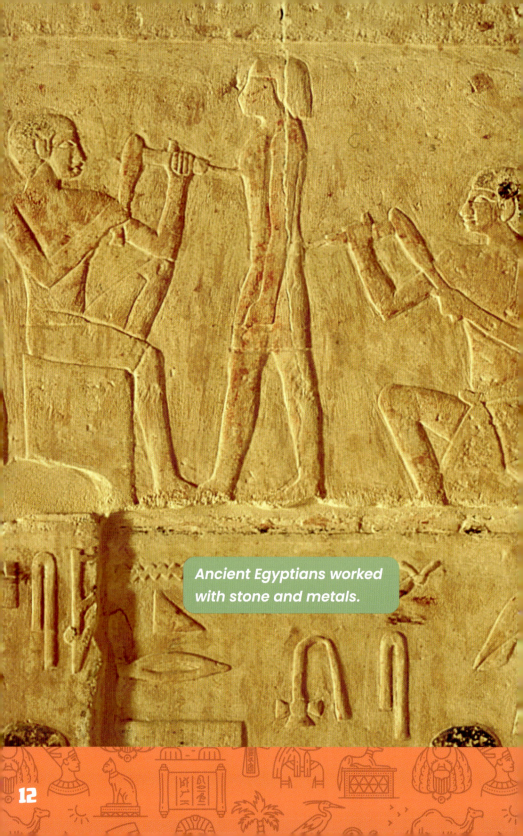

Ancient Egyptians worked with stone and metals.

Scientists believe that ancient Egyptians used copper **chisels** to shape the Sphinx. The workers used stone hammers too. Scientists say it would likely have taken three years for about 100 men to shape the Sphinx.

MISSING SOMETHING

When Egyptians completed the Great Sphinx, it had a small beard. **Pharaohs** like Khafre often wore fake beards. They **symbolized** royalty. But there is no beard on the Sphinx today. Now, parts of the Sphinx's beard are in museums.

Scientists have also found bits of paint on the Sphinx. They think the head covering used to be yellow and blue.

The Great Sphinx is a huge **statue**. In fact, it is one of the largest statues in the world.

The Sphinx is 66 feet (20 m) high. This is about as tall as two telephone poles. And, the Sphinx is 240 feet (73 m) long. That is as long as a jumbo jet!

Giraffe
20 feet (6 meters) tall

Person
5 to 6 feet
(1.5 to 1.8 meters) tall

SIZE COMPARISON

The Great Sphinx is not as tall as the **pyramids** near it. But, it is still big. It would take about 11 people standing on each other's shoulders to reach the top of the Sphinx's head. The craftsmen who carved the Sphinx's face had to be careful not to fall.

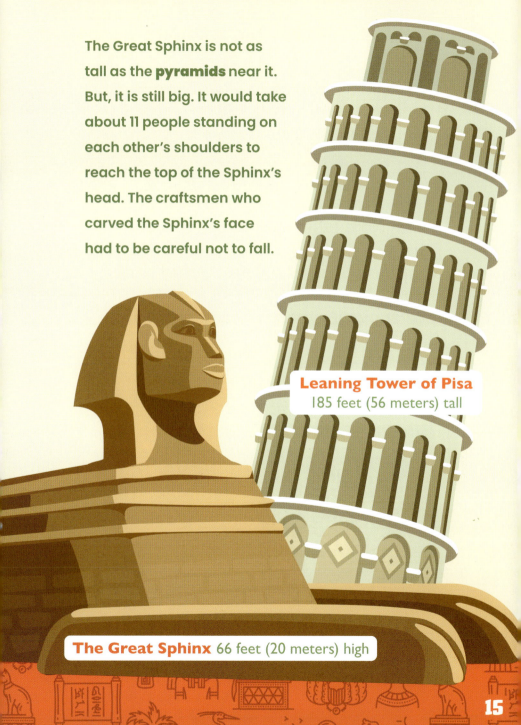

Leaning Tower of Pisa 185 feet (56 meters) tall

The Great Sphinx 66 feet (20 meters) high

CHAPTER 3
SPHINXES RULE

There were other sphinxes in ancient Egypt too. Sphinxes were signs of rulers' power over Egyptians. Many **pharaohs'** heads were on sphinxes.

COMPLETE AN ACTIVITY HERE!

People can see this sphinx at the Metropolitan Museum of Art in New York.

One sphinx with a pharaoh's head is in a New York museum. This sphinx has the head of Hatshepsut. She was one of only a few female pharaohs. People first found the **statue** in an Egyptian temple honoring Hatshepsut.

Sphinxes often appear in Egyptian art. They can have the head of a human,

At least five other sphinxes were in Hatshepsut's temple.

The sphinxes of Karnak Temple have rams' heads.

ram, or hawk. A road connecting temples in Karnak and Luxor has many sphinxes along it. It is known as Sphinx Alley.

The face of the Great Sphinx no longer has a nose.

Ancient Egyptians believed many of their pharaohs were partly **divine**. So, a sphinx with the head of a ruler also had divine properties. This includes the Great Sphinx.

Late in ancient Egyptian history, a Muslim man saw people **worshipping** the Great Sphinx. Muslims practice a monotheistic religion. They believe people should worship only one god, Allah. The man did not like seeing people praying to something else. So, he had some people break off the Sphinx's nose!

DID YOU KNOW? Egyptians worshipped many gods. They ruled over both nature and everyday life.

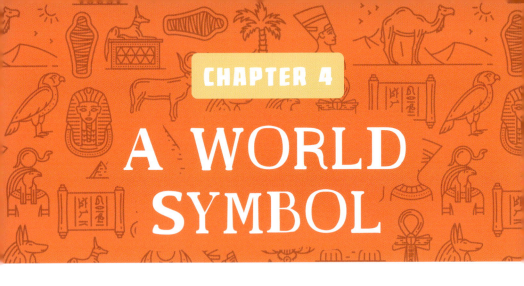

CHAPTER 4
A WORLD SYMBOL

The Great Sphinx has been around for about 4,500 years. During that time, it has become famous around the world. Some societies even borrowed the idea of the sphinx from Egypt.

LEARN MORE HERE!

The Sphinx of Naxos is an ancient Greek statue.

This Hittite sphinx carving is in Turkey.

Egyptian people were the first to create sphinxes. But their idea spread to other areas. Asian societies began to create their own editions of the Egyptian sphinx. Asian sphinxes had lion bodies. But many also had wings.

Greek people also had their own version of the sphinx. They probably learned about the sphinx from people in Asia. In a famous Greek tale, a sphinx asks people a riddle. If they get the riddle wrong, the sphinx eats them!

The Great Sphinx is a global sign of power and Egyptian society. People want it to stand for as long as possible. Laborers have worked to **restore** it several times. In 2007, workers used pumps to save the Sphinx from water rising underground. With help like this, the Great Sphinx could survive for another thousand years or more.

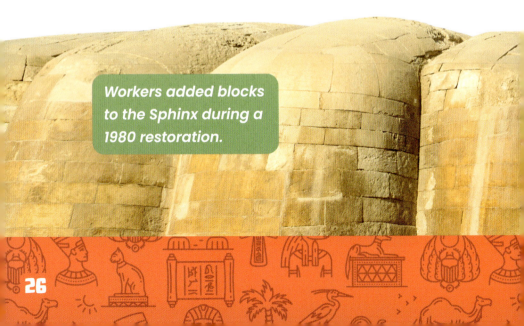

Workers added blocks to the Sphinx during a 1980 restoration.

DIG DEEPER
WITH THE GREAT SPHINX

Androsphinx
- Head of a human
- Body of a lion

Criosphinx
- Head of a ram
- Body of a lion

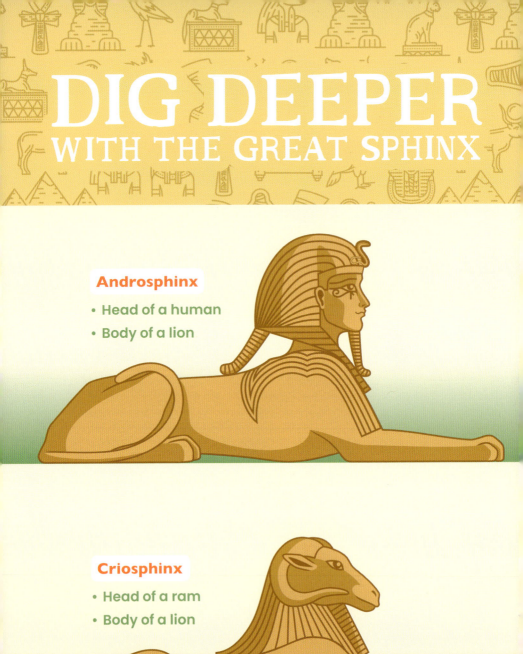

SPHINXES OF ALL SHAPES

Egyptian sphinxes came in several types. The best known is the androsphinx. It has a human head. The criosphinx has a ram's head. The ram is connected to the god Amon. A hieracosphinx was in the Temple of Ramses II.

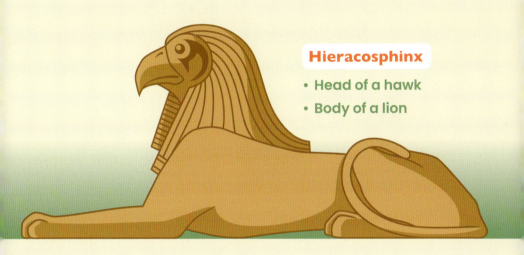

Hieracosphinx
- Head of a hawk
- Body of a lion

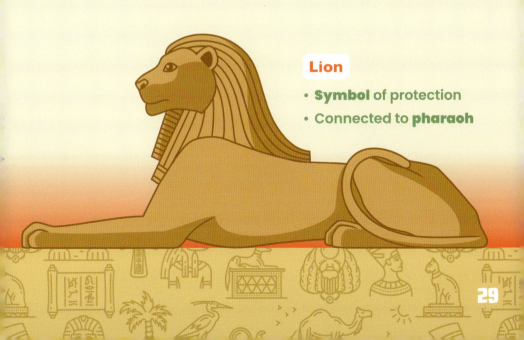

Lion
- **Symbol** of protection
- Connected to **pharaoh**

MAKING CONNECTIONS

TEXT-TO-SELF

Would you be interested in visiting the Great Sphinx? Why or why not?

TEXT-TO-TEXT

Have you read other books about ancient statues or art? How do those books compare with this one?

TEXT-TO-WORLD

What are some important statues you have seen? Do they have special meanings? If so, what do they mean? If not, what other purpose do the statues have?

GLOSSARY

chisel — a metal tool with a handle and a sharp edge for shaping stone, wood, or metal.

divine — having to do with or being a god.

pharaoh — the highest ruler in ancient Egypt.

pyramid — a structure with a square base and four triangular sides that create a pointed top.

restore — to bring back to an earlier, better condition.

statue — a work made of solid material such as stone, usually to look like something else.

symbolize — to stand for a person, place, or thing. Something that does this is a symbol.

tomb — a place where people bury or put their dead, usually to honor them.

worship — to give praise and honor to a god or goddess.

INDEX

Asia, 9, 25

Giza, 4, 8–9

Greece, 9, 25

Hatshepsut, 18

Karnak, 19

Khafre, 7–9, 13

limestone, 10

Luxor, 19

New York, 18

pyramid, 4, 8–9, 15

religion, 20–21

restoration, 26

ONLINE RESOURCES
popbooksonline.com

Scan this code* and others like it while you read, or visit the website below to make this book pop!

popbooksonline.com/great-sphinx

*Scanning QR codes requires a web-enabled smart device with a QR code reader app and a camera.